Atrocities at Camp Mauthausen

Atrocities at Camp Mauthausen

A Visual Documentation of the Holocaust

Schiffer Military History
Atglen, PA

Printed in China.
ISBN: 0-7643-1777-6

We are always looking for people to write books on new and related subjects. If you have an idea for a book, please contact us at the address below.

Published by Schiffer Publishing Ltd.
4880 Lower Valley Road
Atglen, PA 19310
Phone: (610) 593-1777
FAX: (610) 593-2002
E-mail: Info@schifferbooks.com.
Visit our web site at: www.schifferbooks.com
Please write for a free catalog.
This book may be purchased from the publisher.
Please include $3.95 postage.
Try your bookstore first.

In Europe, Schiffer books are distributed by:
Bushwood Books
6 Marksbury Ave.
Kew Gardens
Surrey TW9 4JF
England
Phone: 44 (0)20 8392-8585
FAX: 44 (0)20 8392-9876
E-mail: Bushwd@aol.com.
Free postage in the UK. Europe: air mail at cost.
Try your bookstore first.

Introduction

Social science, and history in particular, has become the object of discussion by people pro- and anti- "revisionist history." But whatever approach one chooses to take, good historians still rely on written records of the period they study. The inclusion and exclusion of people – in power or marginalized – is pivotal to our understanding of the times.

This remarkable reprint contains two first hand accounts about events in camps during World War II – both by people who may be seen as marginalized in some ways. The first is by Franz Ziereis who narrates some of his experiences as commandant of Concentration Camp Mauthausen. It is combined with a narrative by Charles-Heinz Pilarski, a soldier in the German army who was court-martialed and imprisoned in *Feldstraflager* I.

John Beatty, Ph.D.
Professor of Anthropology
Brooklyn College, Brooklyn, NY

THE DEATH HOUSE

FORWARD.

This booklet is composed of two ports. First —
the confessions of Franz Ziereis, Commander of
the infamous Concentration Camp Mauthausen.
Secondly, — The slory of Charles Pilarski, a
Political Prisoner of the Nazi 4 Years.

This is the Last Examination Document of the
Confessions of the Former Camp Commander,
Mauthausen, Standartenführer,Franz Ziereis.

————ooooo————

HOW HE WAS SHOT.

On the 23 May I was hit from the bullets of an American patrol while I was trying to flee. This happened in the vicinity of Spittal on the River Pyrrn. My name is Franz Ziereis, born on August 8, 1905. I was commander of Camp Mauthausen and the adjoining camps. While fleeing I was shot in the left arm in the back. The bullets hit my ventral. I was delivered to the 131st evacuation hospital, (American) at Gusen. I am now willing to state all that I know and the atrocities that have occured.

METHODS TO KILL PRISONERS.

By order of the Reichsminister, Himmler, I was to kill all the prisoners by orders of the Obergruppenführer, Dr. Kaltenbrunner. The prisoners were to be crowded into a long like cave in one of the quarry walls. The opening to be walled up with lar rocks. Then I was to set dynamite at the entrance and blow it up I refused these orders. This was for the prisoners of Camp Guse I and II.

METHODS OF GASSING THE PRISONERS.

In Camp Mauthausen, a gas chamber was built by secret orders of SS-Hauptsturmführer, Dr. Krebsbach, It was camoflauged with all types of shower fixtures. Inside the room the prisoners were gassed by a disinfecting gas, called Cyklon-Bi. Another ingeneous method was to place the prisoners in a truck that travel

This is the stone quarry where they worked the prisoners. The steps in the background (185) in all. The prisoners were required by means of whips of the foremen to carry huge stones (50 kg) the full length.

Gas Chamber. This is the room where the SS eliminated those who were no longer of any use to them. The room is approximately 20 Ft. by 20 and here they crowded in about one hundred and fifty people. Telling them, that they would have a hot shower, but there was no water. At this time, they released gas and killed them all.

Entrance to the Gas-Chamber: The door is about 4 inches thick to prevent the people from breaking out. As when overcome from the gas they gain much strength. The illustrater is the author Charles Pilarski.

ed between Camp Mauthausen and Gusen, and Gusen, and give them Carbon monoxide gas. This idea was brought out by the druggist, SS Ustuf Waschitzki. I never had had a share in this type of killing. I only drove the truck at times. However I knew the prisoners were being gassed inside. All I had were killed by us were by orders of the Reichsicherheitsamt, or Himmler, Heydrich, or Dr. Kaltenbrunner, head of the "Police of Security" of my group.

KILLING AT CAMP GUSEN.

"Details about the last 800 prisoners who were slain at Gusen, with axes and whips, I can't fully remember. I never gave the orders for this last incident. I also don't know about the 640 prisoners who were gassed by the German block masters, Fliegel and Tuelung. These two people are dead now. This happened in Gusen Block 37. The orders were given by camp commander Seidler and Rapportführer Killemann. In case the blockmasters refused to obey the orders the prisoners were not to leave the camp alive. I know nothing about Oberscharf. Zentsch, who killed about 700 prisoners in Gusen by giving them a cold "hose shower" for many hours during the winter days, while the temperature was 12 degrees below freezing."

A scene in the court-yard: Here they eliminated many by giving them a ice cold shower in severely cold weather.

INJECTIONS OF POISON.

"I cannot tell you where Dr. Kaltenbrunner sought refuge
He killed some 700 prisoners by injecting 40 cc near the veins o
their heart. Dr. Richter did his type of killing by operating the
prisoners in the brain. Also by doing same to the stomach of
the sick. Or if slightly sick he would take out the kidney and
liver. I sent him into the "InternalCamp" of Gunskirchen. He was
to take charge of the inmates there. I also did not know that
the Unterscharführer, Miroff, of Peggau Camp killed 15 prisoners
because they were sick. Orders from Berlin were to flog the slav
to death. I did that often myself, getting enjoyment in hearing
them cry out when I struck them on their "asses".

GLUCKS KILLED MILLIONS OF PEOPLE.

The sick and feeble people were ordered by Pohl to be
driven into woods of the vicinity of the camps and gather berrie
Pohl was ordered to cut the portions from 750 grams to 350 weekl
Gruppenführer Glucks ordered all feeble prisoners to be treated
insane and to be gassed in a very convenient place. The place wa
to be Hartheim which is about 10 Km from Linz, in the direction
of Passau. Here about one and one half million people have been
killed. In this camp all prisoners were listed as being gassed b
on official record they died of "normal death". Those who were
still alive were transported to Camp Gusen I, where they were lis
ed as "Political Prisoners".

GLUCKS ACCUSED OF CONSTRUCTING THE GAS CHAMBERS.

"I should like to meet up with the Reichsführer SS Himmler and Obergruppenführer Glucks and Pohl. The whereabouts of the last two I believe I know. I am sure they are at St. Albrecht in the Lorenz. This is a four hour walk up the mountains. The gas chambers in camp Mauthausen were built by orders of Glucks. He assumed that gassing the prisoners was more human than shooting them. One day I was called by the Obergruppenführer Pohl. A transport of 6,000 women and children had come in. They had travelled 10 days without any food or supplies. They were transported in the wintry days of Dec. 1943 in open coal railway cars, without any blankets for shelter. By supreme orders from Berlin, I was to evacuate these women and children to Camp Bergen-Belsen near Hanover. There I, suppose they all met death. This order accounted for my nervous collapse. Another transport arrived with 2500 prisoners from Camp Auschwitz (Upper-Silesia) and come into Camp Mauthausen. These people were tortured by means of the "hose bath" with cold water out in the open cold air. Then, I was to send them to Gusen with only their shorts as protective clothing. This process was repeated many times. The Gauleiter Eigruber, always refused to give food to the new arrivals. He ordered me to deliver only 50 % of the potatoes to be used during the winter months."

ALL WITNESSES OF KILLINGS TO BE KILLED.

"Glucks gave orders that all prisoners working as hangmen at the Mauthausen crematories were to be liquidated at different times when the change of personnel was made. These same men had been in Camp Auschwitz and could give out plenty information if captured by the Allies. An order was given to shoot all hangman and change them every 3 weeks. The same order was given for the prisoner doctors and the occupants of the hospital. I refused to follow these orders. These orders were given for all SS doctors of the hospital by SS Standartenführer, Solling. When I heard this I forbade the order of killing the staff. When I was atrocity camp commander I governed the following camps.

CAMP	AMOUNT OF PRISONERS
Mauthausen	18,000
Gusen, I & II	24,000
Linz, I, II, III	11,000
Ebensee	12,000
Passau I, II, III	810
Fernberg	5,000
Groß-Remning	3,000
Melk	10,000
Eisenerz	5,000
St. Lambrecht	350
Schloß-Lindt	20
Peggau I	500
Peggau II	600
Klagenfurt Junkerschule	200
Laibach	500

CAMP	AMOUNT OF PRISONERS
Lobelpaß	2,000
Lobelpaß-Nord	1,000
Henkelwerke Schwechat	4,000
Wiener Neustadt	1,500
Mistelbach	1,000
Wiener Neudorf	3,000
Floridsdorf	1,000
Henkelwerke-Floridsdorf	800
Sauerwerke (Wien)	2,000
Steyr-Municholtz	3,000
St.Valentine	1,500
Wels	2,000
Amstetten	3,000
Gunskirchen	450

There were many more which I cannot think of at present. Very interesting it was to observe the Jewish prisoners with high professions. They had much counterfiet money and passes and other documents which they had used abroad. This was in camp Schlier."

TRANSPORTING AND TREATMENT OF THE JEWS.

"With Baldur - Schirach and others I received orders from Himmler. All Jews working in the Southeast portion of the front lines are to walk to Mauthausen. Himmler ordered 60,000 Jews to walk to Camp Mauthausen. Only a fraction reached the destination. Of the 4500 Jews transported from the East to Mauthausen, only 180 were alive when they arrived at the station. The transports consisted of women and children and they had no clothing and were sick and feeble. Such transports carried many families who were shot totally on the way to the camp. (At this point Ziereis lied about the treament). The Jews had been starved as badly if not worse than many other victims. (This point was brought out by one survivor who is in Camp Mauthausen Today.) A Jewish transport left for Gunskirchen, about 4 km from Camp Mauthausen, with about 800 dead bodies lying along the roadside. Many trucks were used to pick up the

ZIEREIS FORTUNE.

"My fortune amounts to 13,000 Reichmarks which I have in two different banks. (He affirms he never had any of the precious gold) All documents and pictures I received from Himmler I was to burn. The people working in the Messerschmidt Works only received 8 marks daily per man or women. Only half a mark went to the state for its upkeep."

A BROTHEL FOR THE PRISONERS.

"In order to prevent the prisoners from having intercourse with each other a brothel was built. This was a barrack which held ill famed women for the purpose intended. This house existed for the last six months of Camp Mauthausen fame before the Americans.

This is where the prisoners disembarked on arrival at
Camp Mauthausen and the dress of this Polish is the
same as all people that arrive at this camp.

came in. The men paid 20 Reichmarks for having intercourse with the
prostitute. Of this amount the girl received only 5 marks. The
central concentration camp in Oranienburg commanded by Pohl got 15
marks. The steward of Munich often arranged the drinking parties
in which the prisoners becomeen volved with their women. In order to
get rid of them they acoused them of stealing. So they resolved to
flee from further atrocities. The house at Munich was disbanded
and the prisoners came back to Mauthausen. When they arrived they
committed suicide by throwing themselves against the electric fense.
Bachmayer seeing this called on his large dog who would bite them
to death. The prisoners were doing so because they had been acoused
of circumstances not known, or true".

EXECUTION OF 38 AUSTRIANS ON 29 April 1945.

"I do not know the reason for killing the Austrians as
they bad been arrested for one year and had met death by orders
recieved from the supreme commander "Gauleiter Eigruber". A special
agent of the "gestapo", Prohaska, brought up the execution orders
from Linz with a Gestapo employee of Mauthausen". "Impulsed by the
former leader of the "Political Department", Schulz, The execution
was to take place during the night of 28 April 1945. Finally after
much postponement it took place one night, headed by the ill-famed
Hauptscharführer, Spatzenegger. He was accompanied by the SS of the
camp headquarters.

EXECUTION OF 38 AUSTRIANS ON 29 APRIL 1945 (CONTD).

"Each member of the SS party had machine pistols. The Austrians were brought to the camp office. One got away by the name of Dietel. He succeeded in hiding in the laundry building. The Austrians were lead into the prison building and were shot to death in mass by two "Blockführer" (SS) with machine pistols".

SS-TROOPS CAPTURE AMERICAN OFFICERS:

"One day in Croatia, SS patrols succeeded in capturing a few American officers. They were brought to Camp Mauthausen. There they were accused of being connected with Tito's army. The officers were tortured in various manners". Ziereis, at this point attempted to blame Bachmayer for the above tortures.

MAKING PRISONERS CONFESS.

"The Tibetanian Prayer was used for the first time. The prisoners would confess easily by this method. They would tell all they knew so as to be spared from future torture. The so-called prayer was 3 sticks round or flat which were placed in between the fingers as the prisoner stretched his hands. The SS interrogator would press as hard as he wished. The louder the victim yelled, the more pressure he would put on the sticks. I was very seldom present at such torture. The orders came from Berlin by Zacschke".

HIDING PLACES OF THE VARIOUS SS MEMBERS.

"Obersturmführer Schulz is in Liezen. Lt Obersturmführer
Streitwieser, in Weinzierl and Stauber at Press in Germany". Miss
Embacher, pharmacist, Obersturmführer, Waschitzki live in the house
of Dr. Walter Zechrer in Goisern at Salzburg. Living here also is
the "Labor-Service-Leader", Trumm. The leader of the administrative
duties of Camp Mauthausen, Strauss, is hiding with his family in a
summer house near Kelffenberg, not far from Freistadt. This house
belongs to the torturer, Schepelski, who gassed 160 Russians in
Camp Gusen with poison gas, in Block 16. Orders for killing them
were given by SS Krebsbach and the former Schmielkowski. Schmielkoms-
ki was appointed camp commander in occupied Holland. Here, he was
drunk most of the time and killed prisoners for no reason at all.
His work was so tortureous, that he was taken out of the SS organization. This was done because he had been taking gold, clothes and
many other things of value from the prisoners. In one of his casinos,
he assembled some female prisoners, whipped and violenced them. This
was too much to bear so he was condemmod for 15 years in penal ser-
vitude, plus the fact he had published a paper, which ridiculed the
SS leaders. The sentence was lifted by Himmler himself. He was taken
away and disappeared for other duties maybe. His successor was Grune-
wald, who had been condemned to death for having placed 40 women in
a cell and suffocating them. Himmler also gave orders to release
this man and give him his new duty. Altfuldisch is now a prisoner

in Camp Mauthausen, Streitwieser will be found in Goisern with
SS Stabsführer, Struller and Scharführer von Lammn, a women secretary, from Schlier. I can't remember the hiding place of SS Kluge.
His wife is a cousin of Sturmbannführer Peterseil, first district
inspector of the upper Danube. The family comes from St.Georgen.In
the Watcheneck-Mountains, the place where I was captured, you may
find both district leaders, Eigruber and Peterseil, Holzinger and
lady Kahl, a secretary. For the balance whereabouts of the SS men
and all,please call on my wife Mrs. Ziereis who is now living with
Mrs.Müller,wife of the SS Müller, in the Linzer-hut on Pyrrn-
mountain.

ZIEREIS LETTER TO HIS WIFE:

Ziereis asks to have his wife brought to him if possible.
Time was short so he asks to have a letter written to her.

THE LETTER.
My Dear Wife,
On 23 May, the day you had gone to the store for the
family, I was captured by an American patrol. Behind a tree, 4 km
from the hut, I laid down my machine pistol.
I ask you to tell the examinors everything you know.
Tell them with vivid description of my Berlin superiors and try
to elucidate my refusal of their orders.-- You know our intentions,
where, we would rather die than have our children go through the
acts, that many died in the various camps. I shocked myself when
I was forced to lay down my pistol, due to the severe wounds. After
being hit three times, I remained on the ground. I am in the American 131st Evacuation Hospital at Gusen I. In spite of my injury,

I am able to tell all I can remember. Please, come, and tell
the commissioned examinors about the bad things and behaviour of
the Berlin superiors, including Himmler. Also do not forget the
many things Pohl did".

SINCERELY YOURS,
Your loving husband,
Franz.

FUSSIAN OFFICERS GOT NECK SHOTS:
(Ziereis continues with more gasping of the breath)
"About other camps, I can give you a little detail. In
1941, all Atrocity commanders of Germany were assembled in Berlin,
being advised the best method of liquadating Politrucks and Russians. The leaders decided to demonstrate in Camp Sachenhausen.
Here, they called the prisoners with a loud speaker and lead them
into a long barrack in the far end of the Camp. As each one would
enter the dark gangway, they received a shot in the neck by an SS
who was drunk and disorderly. Each SS man took turns in the shooting. These men were Glück's staff. After shooting the prisoners
some SS men would pile the corpses in 2 big heaps Near the corpses
were two incinerators that burned day and night. They burned 1500
to 2000 daily. This proceeded for five weeks. In Gross-Rosen Camp,
poison was injected into the hearts of the victims. They were
told, this was to help them regain their health".

In this corner they told the prisoners that they would photograph them for some purpose, but instead they shot them. A fake camera was placed where this picture was taken.

Entrance to crematory. This is the entrance which led
from the court-yard to the crematory.

The Cremastory: In this furnace, they burned six to eight bodies at one time. They had three ovens which they kept running day and night. One furnace was capable of burning thirty-six bodies in ten hours.

Under way for cremating.

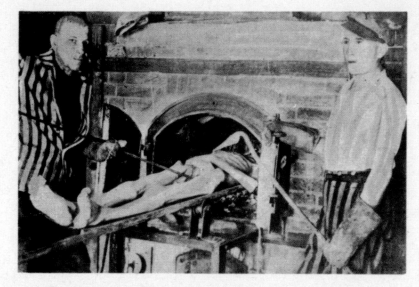

Days and nights the incinerators were kept on
firing . . .

This is the legal form with which they tried to conceal their crimes. One of these accompanied each body which was cremated.

PLUNDERING JEWS AT CAMP BUCHENWALD.

"The plundering was done by Hachmann and Mayer. Mayer was a distant relative of Himmler. They would get all the valuables from the Jews. They had a priceless truck and wore many silken shir and good suits. The Buchenwald arresting inspector would go to Erfurt,(Thuringia) with naked women and make money on the way. Many times he gambled his money that belonged to Hachmann and Mayer. As time went on, his losses were too great and gave nothing to the men he was working for. Not having the correct excuse and knowing all the affairs of the family life of his superiors, he was shot to death. Camp commander Koch had a case of Syphilis and was attended by a prisoner doctor. The doctor was later killed by an SS pharmicist, as the commander thought he had not been given a cure. The SS sold blankets for 100 Reichmarks, yet they were only worth 32 marks

PRISONERS SUSPECTED TO BE INSANE.

"The former SS Camp physician, Sturmbannführer,Dr.Kirchner,killed a lot of prisoners, under the known supposition of "intellectuel inferiority". This killing grew up to a huge atrocity in all camps. It was supported by the state law that governed hereditary diseases, par,74,F13. SS Dr.Lohnauer,had his private practice in Linz as a psychiatrist. He had a commissioned officer in Berlin who mustered the prisoners out of the concentration camps. These prisoners were listed as "Intellectual Inferiors" and sent to the hospital of Hartheim, near Linz". At this point,Ziereis begins to deny the amount of people killed and many other answers to

the many questions, that were thrown at him by the Intelligence
Department. I estimate that about 20,000 prisoners were gassed
within 1 1/2 years that Hartheim was established. This also includes the insane people. I have seen the documents stored in the cell-
ars. It was poison gas from the coal that killed many victims. The
so called gas chambers were pretty well tiled to represent a shower-
room. I would like to say that the SS are not to blame for all the
many atrocities, rather the Police Officers did all the work. I
don't know the captain's name of the police force. I believe he was
killed in Croatia.

"The ashes of the burnt corpses were stored up and gathered behind hospital. When a huge pile was on hand, in order to erase
all indication of burning, the ashes were hauled and dumped into
the Dachau river".

RELATIVES OF DEAD PRISONERS RECEIVE LETTERS OF CONDOLENCE.

"The different camps wrote many letters of condolence
which was finally stopped by Adolph Hitler himself. He put a stop
to the fact, the people would give out with sloppy information
concerning their relatives. In camp Auschwitz, it has and was the
special deputy of the Reichsführer SS, who controlled all gold
transports. He embezzled about 40 Kilos or better than 80 pounds
of gold taken from human teeth. I don't know the name of them, but
I am sure, SS Glücks may know. In all Camps the prisoners, men and
women had their/cropped short by orders. The hair was gathered for
hair

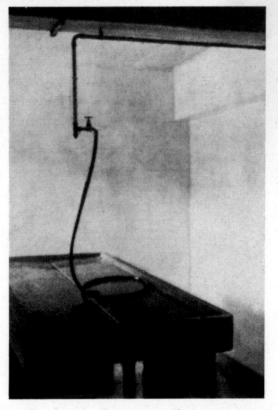

The Cutting Room: In this room they removed all gold and silver from the bodies and prepared them for burning.

insulating felt-boots for the German army. The now killed SS
leader Heydrich, ordered all prisoners to have a cross marked on
their heads with ink pencil so that when cropping time came around
they would not be missed. There was no tattoeing done in Camp
Mauthausen. In Camp Auschwitz, the tattoeing of the numbers on the
prisoners was ordered by the Camp Commanders Hosch and Glücks."
Here, Ziereis denies, that he had not given the orders to keep people
outside in the nude and have them freeze. From 1942 to 43 about a
thousand prisoners were transported from Holland to Camp Mauthausen."

HIMMLER'S INSPECTION OF MAUTHAUSEN CAMP.

"On the 31st of May 1943, Reichsminister Himmler, inspect-
ing the quarries ordered the Jews to carry big granite stones weighing 50 kilos or 100 pounds, up the 185 stone steps. These stones
were to be used in building the camp wall. Many prisoners would vol-
untarily jump over the cliff, so as to escape future tortures. I
tried to tell Himmler that were loosing too many people like that,
and that civilians would notice the people working to death. My
superiors wrote to me and stated that I was to follow every order
given by Himmler regardless of the method to be perscribed".

SUPERIORS OF BERLIN DEMANDED MORE PEOPLE KILLED.

"Three months later, a transport of 7,000 Czechoslovakian
Jews arrived in Camp Mauthausen. The death rate amongst the transport
was only 3 % and was very suspiciously objected by the Berlin superiors. I was questioned about this situation and I replied that I
needed people to work and could not kill them all. In spite of all
these reproaches, I was appointed "Standartenführer".

A scene from the balcony of the hospital looking into the court-yard.

PROMINENT PRISONERS OF CAMP MAUTHAUSEN.

"The son of Horthy, the Hungarian General, lived here under the name of "Mouse"; Badoglio called himself "Brausewetter" and "Cortey" kept his family name. According to orders received from "District-Leader", Eigruber, they were to be shot, but I refused to follow the order. After consulting Colonel Kuppert, I sent them all to Camp Dachau, except Cortey who had hidden himself in the prison bunker. He was fed secretly by the SS kitchen personnel".

"At last in concluding my confession and examination, I state that within the area of Warsaw, Kowno, Riga, and Libau about 16,000000 people were killed .

-.-.-.-.-.-.-.-.-

This document was translated from its German version by a former inmate of this camp, Charles Heinz-Pilarski.

---ooo---

" MY IMPRISONMENT" IN FELDSTRAFLAGER I, 1st COMPANY.

FINLAND-NORWEGIA 6th June 1942-10th Jan. 1943

By Charles-Heinz Pilarski

"This my life's history in the horrible German camps and the extent of the cruelity inflicted upon me".

My life was a thorny episode through Germany's prisons and concentrations-camps. There I was alive in seeing and suffering under cruel whips of fascist education. It was on the 8th of May that I was liberated from the knot of the fanatic hangman by the good fortune of the Americans.

A German Soldier Gets Court-Martialled.

My fault! "Meo Culpa!" ─── The greatest fault, I made in my life was when going to the Army (German) on the 4 th day of November 1937 as a volonteer. Iwent to the airforce in order to acomplish the 2years of compulsary military duty and service brought on to every male member of Germany. In 1939, when war broke out, I was not discharged from the army but was forced to take up arms against Poland and the Allies, Later on. This last circumstance however had been prevented by the will of fate.

In Erfurt, Thuringia, on the 20 th of February 1940, I was court─

"LIVING CONDITIONS IN CAMP MAUTHAUSEN"

"The Quaranteen"

It is thoruoughly emphazised that the so called quaranteen was not only for medical purposes, but for brutal treatments as well.

The length of quarantee varied, according to the room needed by the camp for other victims. It is a known fact that the many prisoners would be in the quaranteed barracks from several days to one year.

The men slept on hay-filled mattresses which were placed on the floor crowded every inch of floor space. The prisoners were arranged like sardines in a can. There were six men to a straw-bed with only two blankets to keep them warm. Two blankets for all six men.

Conditions were crowded both outside the quarters and in, so the „barracks staff" ordered the victims to constantly remain inside on their beds. The men were forced to lay on their sides; this insured the criminal beaters, a better chance to whip and flog the prisoners who lying on the beds created a level surface. The men hug each other closely and could not attempt to get up when the whip or flogging pole came their way. This was not enough so the „barracks staff", men with criminal records, would trod on the poor victims who lay there helpless. Many died within a few hours and days of this rough, cruel and inhuman treatment.

By the translator, **Charles-Heinz Pilarski.**

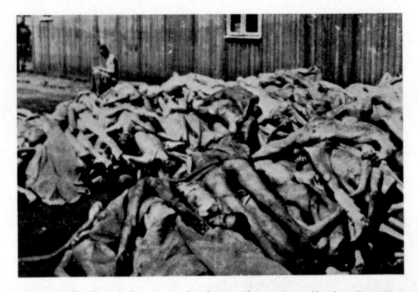

Heap of dead bodies before the so-called „Russian Hospital". They all could be nursed back to life but instead, they starved with hunger, for food to be given to them was small and scanty.

Content of a truck, coming from the „Hospital". Daily scene before the crematory-entrance.

Senselessly they piled up the Death-bodies.

Slain Russian prisoners of war.

The hanging of Polish civilians who would no longer keep out the tortures, tried to escape.

Russian prisoners awaiting attention which never came.

martialed. There, I was reproached with anti-fascistic agitation
among the ranks of soldiers that was equal to the decomposition of
the military forces. The trial nearly lasted four hours.

I was sentenced to 3 years of military prison for circumstances
which if furnished in a civilian court,it would be thrown out because
they were small facts. The punishment was to be put into force after
the end of the war,if Germany had won.Elp to   time,I was to remain
in a concentration camp. As all cells were over crowded, I was brought
from the Prison of Remand to the well known military prison,the anc-
ient   fortress on the River Elbe,called Torgau.

Behind The Latticed Windows Of The Fortress Torgau On The Elbe River.

It was on the 20 April 1940, Herr Hitler's birthday,I was taken to
the fortress at Torgau. What honor. . I thought they would stop transporting prisoners on this day. I was always accompanied by two serg-
eant-majors of the Luftwaffe, I went on to the direction of Torgau.

Torgau was a newly built prison consisting of four large buildings,
six stories high. Inside were more than 1,000 lonely cells.These
buildings were arranged in a cross form so that one could observe
what action was taking place from one building to another.There was
food in the large fortress. Yes! Food, but not for the prisoners.
The fortress finally filled up with more than 3,000 victims of inno-
cent circumstances.

At Torgau, we didn't enjoy for a long time our life behind latticed
windows, "God be praised",this state of useless staring against
white painted walls without doing any work. It was too good to be
true not to work, we thought. Reading and writing was strictly out.
Soon,all this found an end. In spite of the restrictions,many did
so and were severly punished. I did it too. It cost me the price of
a seven day arrest, locked in a dark cell. The food given me amoun-
ted to 600 gramms of dried bread and cold water.

The daily life at Torgau consisted of military exercises and monve -
ments without the use of any weapons. One day,early in the morning,all
prisoners were assembled in the courtyard. The prison commander,Oberst
Remmlinger,began to speak.He spoke quote,"Up to the next coming
weeks you are to work for Germany's fortifications,extending from the
Biscaya to the Polar Sea.Within a measurable space of time you get
transportation and about 500 prisoners at once will go to the Artic,
where you have to work in quarries under the influence of the enemy's
bombardment". Unquote.

With the "Death" Battallion To The Arctic.

To the Artic we were taken. The 6th of June 1942 begon our voyage.We
were placed into trucks and busses thoroughly and completely crowd-
ed.The windows were railed with barbed-wire,that flight might be
prevented.Thus we reached the port of Danzig.Here,we were placed again in cells on awaiting ships.They always put us in the below water
level decks,so that we could not see or hear a thing.They kept us
from observing the beautiful sea coasts of Finland.After a two day
voyage,we arrived at the sea port of Jacobstadt,a small town in South-
West Finland.After being loaded in waggons and busses again,we arriv-

ed at the railway station and boarded trains awaiting us. Again we were
crowded and finally reached Rovaniemi. The pains of a compresses voyage by rail had finished, but new ones, much greater, awaited us.

A Thorny Way Along The Polar-Sea-Road.

In Rovaniemi now began the 500 km long march to the Norwegian Artic
harbor of Kirkenes. Due to the scorching sun in the North, being the
month of June, we marched only at night. We would march from 30 to
35 km nightly, accompanied by the watching eyes of the Wehrmacht corporals whose baggage naturally were carried by trucks. Not having
enough for us to carry, they thought, we had to carry the equipment of
the Wehrmacht's. These corporals gave us rucksacks, food-bags, gas
masks etc., all weighing about 50 pounds, which they should be carrying.

The march on to the Polar-Sea-Road was in demand of all forces and the
food was very scanty. Many people were getting thin and very feeble.
Others got sores on their feet and couldn't proceed marching onward. They
would set themselves down on the road's banks and remained there for a
spell. Some recovered and continued on, limping. Others, already too feeble,
lay down gasping for breath and couldn't stand up, when the guards
tried to make them continue the march. After the battalion had passed
the ones who had fallen and we were about 300 meters away, we heard
the rifle shots. We knew the guards had made short work of our comrad-
es. Thus, our first casualities began. A few were taken to the hospital,
where little care was given to them and they passed on like the rest.
The battalion was getting smaller daily.

Marching! Marching! One day I had a very severe attack of diarrhoea.
The doctor ordered me to the hospital, as he suspected me of having
an infection of typhus. I was taken by truck, watched by the bloody
eyes of a sergeant-major and taken into the hospital of Ivalo, which
lies in the midst of Finland. In this hospital there were many other
prisoners. All the windows had heavy barbed wire to insure the sick of
flight. In spite of these circumstances however, I believe that the six
weeks, I stayed in the hospital had saved me, at least for the time
being. In the meantime the "Death Battalion" had arrived at Kirkenes.
A distance well over (500 km.)

Hard Work In The Northern Quarries. General Diet'ls Harangue

Work began in the Northern quarries with frigid temperatures. The food
was not getting better, thereby we could not revover from our suffered
fatigues. Winter time was pretty well under way. The light tents were to
be cleared and barracks to be built. The cold increased to forty degrees
below zero. The daily average was about 30 degrees. The clothing was not
sufficient enough to grant a shelter against the cold. Many soldiers
were afflicted with frostbitten feet, nose and ears. New victims of death
and much sickness.

The company commander again spoke to the soldiers. He was a man who lov-
ed to harass the men. His words were quote "The work should be continued under all circumstances" Unquote. This was not enough to make one's
blood boil, so, one day General Dietl, Chief of the Occupied North at the
time, made his speech. He was a stubborn and cruel person. He said, quote
"You are by the will of our Führer, ordered here for hard work in the
quarries, to create a strong base in the rocks. You are to lay the
foundation stone for Germany's fortifications, extending from the Biscaya to the Polar-Sea. Everyone who goes against my orders will be

crushed and punished". Unquote. The fortifications were erected with rocks, yes, bloody ones. The losses were great, for many were unable to accomplish the hard work and refused to march out of the quarry with their working commander. Some only recieved half rations of food or remained in their tents, chained to the hands and feet. Three weeks later, this torture came to an end. The victims were condemmed to death and shot.

Russian Progress in The East, Germans Need Cannon Fodder.

Time went on and nine months later, when all the work was finished, except some infantry bunkers which were cut into the rocks, the food given us was better. They gave us more bread, butter and sugar. Even blubber which in the winter time was very indispensable for this region. I always thought that they were fattening us up for good cannon fodder. Perhaps because of the great losses on the Eastern front in 1943/44, they decided to treat us better, to still win their intentions later. It was too late however. Of the 500 prisoners who had left from Torgau for Kirkenes, only less than half returned. The balance had gotten sick, feeble, starved, or were shot to death on the stony borders of the Polar-Sea-Road. Others again refusef to go on working in the quarries for the work was too hard for them to endure. These people were court-martialled and condemmed to death. Only one percent were able to take flight and to escape the further agony of the Nazis. These went over to Norwegian territory and then escaped on to England.
I hope that today they have been apprehended and questioned as to the atrcities which they so vividly witnessed being inflicted by the cruel system of the Nazis and the Father land who, killing their sons and people meant nothing.
After I left the hospital, I was brought into Camp Mauthausen.

This is a ceremony which took place after the Americans arrive. At this time, there was presented to each country an urn of dirt in commemmoration of those burried here. These urns will be sent to each country in remembrance.

The SS work at the quarry, the table is now turned and they do not give orders, but instead take them.

More SS working as they made the people do when
they were the so call master.

Related titles on the Holocaust

THE CAMP MEN
The SS Officers Who Ran
the Nazi Concentration Camp System
French L. MacLean

Inside these pages you will meet over 960 infamous men – the officers of Nazi Germany's *Totenkopf* (Death's Head). These officers were not the bureaucrats who meticulously planned Adolf Hitler's Final Solution from behind a desk in Berlin, or those who quietly scheduled the trains that carried the victims to the camps. Quite the contrary; these men stood on the front-line of the Nazi war to exterminate the Jews. With well over one hundred photographs–a large portion previously unpublished – this is the largest collection of SS camp personnel photographs ever to appear in one work.
Size: 8 1/2" x 11" • over 140 b/w photos, maps • 384 pp.
ISBN: 0-7643-0636-7 • hard cover • $59.95

THE FIELD MEN
The SS Officers Who Led the Einsatzkommandos –
the Nazi Mobile Killing Units
French MacLean

Men lined up in four motorized columns immediately behind the German Army on June 22, 1941, as it prepared to launch Operation Barbarossa, an attack designed to win the war. The Field Men covers the entire gamut, from the organization of the units, to the SS officers who served in this scourge on the Eastern Front. Some 380 SS officers are described in full detail and extensively analyzed.
Size: 8 1/2" x 11" • over 175 b/w photographs and maps • 232 pp.
ISBN: 0-7643-0754-1 • hard cover • $59.95

THE GHETTO MEN: The SS Destruction
of the Jewish Warsaw Ghetto April-May 1943
French MacLean

The twenty-eight day siege of the Warsaw Ghetto was one of the most protracted large-scale urban battles in World War II. Only the fighting at Leningrad from 1941-1943, Stalingrad in 1942-1943, the Warsaw Rebellion of 1944, and Budapest in 1944-1945 lasted longer. This book presents every fact possible concerning the who, when, with what and how the SS troops razed the Warsaw Ghetto. The men and officers of the dreaded Security Service and Gestapo are here as well as the units, weapons and tactics, and a day-by-day analysis of the fighting.
Size: 8 1/2"x11" • over 110 b/w photos • 224 pp.
ISBN: 0-7643-1285-5 • hard cover • $59.95

THE CAMP WOMEN
The Female Auxiliaries Who Assisted the SS
in Running the Nazi Concentration Camp System
Daniel Patrick Brown

The first complete resource devoted to the *SS-Aufseherinnen* – the female guards of the German concentration camps during World War II. In addition, the role of the girl's youth organization in developing future overseers, and the eventual recruitment, training, and employment of these women is likewise examined. Professor Brown's timely work fills a void in the terrible annals of Nazism: at last, the women guards and their crimes are subject to public scrutiny.
Size: 8 1/2" x 11" • over 50 b/w photographs, documents • 288 pp.
ISBN: 0-7643-1444-0 • hard cover • $59.95

THE CRUEL HUNTERS
SS-Sonderkommando Dirlewanger -
Hitler's Most Notorious Anti-Partisan Unit
French L. MacLean

The Dirlewanger Battalion, also known as "Sonderkommando (special commando) Dirlewanger" was perhaps the least understood, but at the same time the most notorious German SS anti-partisan unit in World War II. Medieval in their outlook on war and certainly not indicative of many German military formations, this unit none-the-less remains a reflection of a segment of mankind gone mad in the inferno of World War II on the eastern front.
Size: 6" x 9" • over 50 b/w photographs, maps • 336 pp.
ISBN: 0-7643-0483-6 • hard cover • $29.95

SS OFFICERS LIST (as of January 1942)
SS-Standartfuhrer to SS-Oberstgruppenfuhrer –
Assignments and Decorations of
the Senior SS Officer Corps.

The January 1942 "Dienstalterliste" lists the hundreds of officers in the SS from full Colonel to General. Detailing their post at that time during the war, this wartime publication, available now for the first time in a facsimile edition, also gives significant decorations they were awarded. Their ranks and most recent promotion dates are listed as well as State, Police and NSDAP posts. Illustrated with more than forty rare photos, this rare publication provides detailed information for historians and militaria collectors. Fully indexed.
Size: 8 1/2" x 11" • over 45 b/w photographs • 64 pp.
ISBN: 0-7643-0061-5 • soft cover • $19.95

IN PERFECT FORMATION
SS Ideology and the SS-Junkerschule-Tölz
Jay Hatheway

Includes extensive references to original source material on the underlying SS principles of blood, soil, and struggle as they were formalized in SS ideology. In support of his intricate linkages between ideology and its realized form, Hatheway has obtained over 100 previously unpublished photos of the SS officer training academy Tölz. More than a series of buildings, the structure of the *Junkerschule* was itself a metaphor for the subset of Nazi ideology that was developed by Himmler, Darré and others to create a racially pure vanguard to lead Germany on its path toward Teutonic regeneration.
Size: 6" x 9" • over 100 b/w photographs • 192 pp.
ISBN: 0-7643-0753-3 • hard cover • $29.95

Dedicated to

Master Sergeant Matthew Jankowski
1918-1969

Who served in the United States Army in World War II. This campaign put an end to the mass slaughter of the Holocaust, the genocide of European Jews and others – a systematic and planned extermination by the Nazis. Matty brought home and preserved from the past this document of hostility and horrific widespread destruction.

Mrs. Lenora J. Jankowski
1918-2001

More than thirty years elapsed after her husband had passed and Lee managed to keep this relic of a bygone era intact. One among many mementos that will keep them both eternally in our minds and hearts.

— Matthew L. Jankowski